HP

Richmond upon Thames Libraries

Renew online at www.richmond.gov.uk/libraries

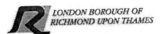
LONDON BOROUGH OF
RICHMOND UPON THAMES

90710 000 471 884

What Fire

Alice Miller

LONDON BOROUGH OF
RICHMOND UPON THAMES

90710 000 471 884

Askews & Holts	12-May-2021
823.92 MIL	
RTHA	

DISCARDED

First published 2021 by
Liverpool University Press
4 Cambridge Street
Liverpool
L69 7ZU

Copyright © 2021 Liverpool University Press

The right of Alice Miller to be identified as the author of this book
has been asserted by her in accordance with the Copyright, Designs
and Patents Act 1988.

All rights reserved. No part of this book may be reproduced, stored
in a retrieval system, or transmitted, in any form or by any means,
electronic, mechanical, photocopying, recording, or otherwise,
without the prior written permission of the publisher.

British Library Cataloguing-in-Publication data
A British Library CIP record is available

ISBN 978-1-800-85962-3 softback

Typeset by Carnegie Book Production, Lancaster
Printed and bound in Poland by Booksfactory.co.uk

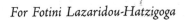

For Fotini Lazaridou-Hatzigoga

I am hush'd until our city be a-fire,
And then I'll speak a little.

Volumnia in *Coriolanus*

Contents

~

Seams

In time all cities blur and connect
as each street remembers
another, remembers the downward
pressure on your temple
as the plane rises, rises, as the lights
of one city are gurgled by fog, and what's left
is one more night between time zones.

What glow here. What unbreakable seams.

You know the earth, like your body, can't take this,
won't last, and yet tonight you need too much to get home.
What else do you need too much?
Another plane slips across darkness
before the cloud shifts and again
a city—its networked wide grids, grips of colour, unreal green
of some outskirts' stadium before black cloud pours back in.

Did you use your time on earth to save
what you wanted? Did you use anyone
the way you should? What song
will you sing as the light leaves,
as the mask's lowered over your eyes?

An Opening

Green lit white on waves.
Churn shines like bit skin. I love
the ocean's utter sinkage,
love how stones travel down slow,
how gulls dive and bring up shells
to toss on rocks and open meat.
Meat's not ours anymore, land's taking itself back.
Animals too. A war like no other's begun
though for now we wouldn't know it.
For now waves lick skin, prop up bodies,
float us over unthinkable depths
out into unthinkable distance.
Lie on the surface and feel the pull,
try to trick the water to answer.

New Wings

Looking out at a man's name on a battered wingtip
in strong winds; was it planned that when
the cheap wing bends, the name stays steady?
What if it didn't matter how much
you trod over the body of your mother, what happened
when you were younger, how you tried forgetting
and forgot to forgive. Something has to
hold you: numbers, columns,
cards to swipe, books to shelve,

pints to pour. A life filled with fixed wings, with hard grasps,
with the grateful. What's worth keeping?
Not the sad boy who blamed you for all the ways he was broken.
Not the man's name on the wing, but
why not the battered wing
itself. Why not the woman thinking.
Why not the river below, its lips wet, footprints animal.
What forked tongues come when clouds crack open,
when this sky's watched you sleep all day, and now
lets down its darkness. There's all night to stay awake.

Awake

This morning you wake to see all towns
are one town, so there's little point in taking
a train or bike or boat to find
a slightly altered face for the same soul.
And not only the towns: the woods are all
the same woods, no divergent twig, no path
that wasn't pre-written into existence by a programme
you've seen so many times before you could recite
each oak, each branch. So where is the hole
in the earth   where you scrape your way out of extinction?
Where is the gift   under the bodies, down where
the burning stops? Does the burning stop?   (Yes!)
This morning you start to dig.

The Goddess of Death

There's a Māori legend they read to us as kids
about the trickster demigod Māui
who decides to defeat death.
He hides from the goddess of death and while she sleeps
he crawls up inside her vagina
to kill her in her sleep.

He's about to become the man who defeats death forever
but instead, because of the chirrup
of a bird, the goddess wakes
and squeezes Māui
to death between her thighs.

You can see why the story stays with you.

Now I guess we're not only crawling up between her thighs
but we're bringing everything we can carry
driving up in our SUVs and our jetplanes
stuffing this woman's vulva full of metal, plastic,

space junk, Primark bikinis and polystyrene
mannequins, clipboards and laptops, parabens
and silicone, we're shovelling it all deep
in her bloodstream,
while she tries to rest, as she's been trying to rest

all these years since Māui woke her.
Still, the stories say she created death.
We will never let her rest.

New Valkyrie

Dear, I would be a terrible chooser
of the dead.

How to keep my eyes clear
while determining

which half lived, which
died—today

a woman I love was told
she had an illness spread

too far to cure. She isn't yet forty.
Why can't we undo it, she said

down the phone.
I'd like to be impartial,

immortal, to seem to consider,
and let her live.

She has a mind
like no one I know.

Dear, let me say something better
than the nothing I utter.

Better yet, let me change this:
Let me shatter each tumour.

A Valkyrie chooses who dies
in battle. The half who die—

the *einherjar*—must prepare
for the world's end,

and sometimes
the Valkyries come

to bring them mead.
Today I am still waiting

to hear from her,
still waiting to get home

to see her. So I will bring her mead,
one way or the other.

Orbit

All caught in cycles of traffic, one woman turning
into full grief, one man stuck at red-lit-denial
and we so softly drifting through the
miraculous section, where the signs are gone
and the hills are endless and
we know we can't stay.
It's what makes it, of course.
I've been above the cloud so much lately
and it doesn't get old, this window.
Clouds don't age. But how
impossible the reckoning of a course that runs circular
and turns to run itself over again. Live and
don't learn. The city loses its verbs,
becomes only buildings. The sea lacks an edge,
breaks through grass. I'm flying hours
to see you, to simplify: my body, called to you, goes.
The sea's turning trees to water.
This breaching is a kind of sky.

The names we call one another
are fissures, gaps. What belongs alongside, what sits together,
what's held open not to let words out, but bright
light in. How to build without faults, to make this house
immune to fire with no emergency switch.
How to trust wood, know steel. It's a feeling I have
says the room, its warmth also damp, its skin also pulsing.
Push here. Where will you live, they ask,
but I know our unknowing can remake
each city where our world is made. We'll die, won't we?
That's part of the walls, the floor, buttons
of coats hanging on hooks beside the broken stairwell.
What's so wide-eyed it's bruising. I want our countries

to know one another,
to switch poles and touch.
I want winter to come over and over and over and
be caught at the window able to tell
what's sea and what's land. What's at hand
is everything. I want to meet you
at the end of my sentence and recognise,
laughing, oh, you've been here all along.

The Woman

Because time was once not rewindable,
we have made it rewindable now. What do you go back
to check on and change? How do you accept the Hell
you make? That night you decided to build the walls,
you stayed up all night regretting their height, a reach
you'd never live up to. What is the point if a poem can't

save us? But something sewn into it
believes it can, the woman raises
a placard on the bridge, and while
these blank faces pass her by, she refuses
to shade the sun's sharp blast
from her eyes' cold sheen.

Two Thousand Years

Here in the snow the horses
stamp, impatient for their carriages
to give way to cars. Impatient

for time to fix itself. *Two thousand
years and change*, a voice calls from
someone else's darkness. Impatient to get past

these leaders we thought impossible, we call
the desert forward, please,
we call for the woman-lion,

we kneel in the sand to welcome
her riddles, we ask
to kiss her burning paws,

if she can just remind us
how to trap time with time
to find what we came here to save.

What Becomes Her

Heaven knows you're tired, dear one, as you walk
along the dappled Spree, watching small crowds obey
the season, order ice-cream, all their steps today
theatrical, as if they know of a far-off
catastrophe and they eat ice-cream to assure
themselves they're still untouchable.

But as there's no new catastrophe, it must be you
seeing their steps differently, you're changed,
bruised—why can't you protect yourself
against the dark thought-scraps that grip you,
against a man who was hit as a child?

One day you'll be rid of him forever.
Look, a leaf-sized bird, twig-legged, a tree
the shape of an octopus. In the middle
of the river, the dapples never still. Three
tossed silver cans lie in a stagnant
slice of water beside a blue boat called STERN.

So, now, reach down
where no one can see you,
let your fingers slowly untie the rope
until the boat edges out, shimmers uncertainly
alone on the river, and you
stand on the shore counting
each of everyone's catastrophes
as you watch the light-dark dapples carry her.

~

The Fork of Five Rivers

Berlin's river we take with us, all the way down
        to the bottom of the world where the man
who invented Erewhon
            had a sheep station and wrote comedies

about Darwin and the Gospels. He called his station Mesopotamia
        by implication bringing two more rivers
to the two that already meet here.

Today, the graveyard in Mesopotamia holds the bodies
        of two ageing rockers
dead in the nineteen eighties and "still rocking"
            beside a woman who drowned trying
to cross a hundred years ago. All dead mid-river.

How many wrong rivers have we met now, then?
Euphrates, Tigris, Rangitata, Forest Creek, and Spree.

Eventually, like the Erewhon man, we had to go back home
        to a place less wild
with a dishwasher and a corner store
            where the closest rivers run through pipes.

And yet (un)still, rivers gasping, grasping,
        rivers grappling for knowledge,
for answers, for water's
            better, often, than words.

A bit of background: I hitched my fate to a man
        from the fjords.
Inexplicable bodies of water. His body's similar:
        knowable, sleek, traceable, deep.

We live in a city far from fjords, oceans, water.
There is only one river and this summer, surging heat.

This morning our river   coughed up a corpse,
bobbed the length   of the river face-up before
          the Polizei fished it out   in Kreuzberg
          beside the office of a new start-up.

I passed by, identified the body; I swear   it was the Erewhon
man returned, choked   out of the nineteenth century
and asked to build a new utopia.

A pity the river would choose him   when he'd come so far.

I ask you now: what kind of utopia will you build?
What sort of non-Hell will it look like?

Concrete or wood, silk or water?
Who will be allowed in, who   turned back?

Whatever your answer, I'm pleased to find you
at this evening's   confluence of the five rivers.

How far we have come already.   Please go through
and find   a seat in the confluence room.

When you pass by at the fork,   don't look too closely
in the mirror,   don't think too deeply about the water.

We each have our own   scheduled   future, drowning.

We each have our own paradise inside
waiting to drown us   from the inside out.

Strange Weather

Were you told what you'd lose? Strange
weather plunged in, *we were warned*, we did
not nothing but nearly,

I took flights all round the world
and back   every year
I bought a dress   and let moths
eat my old ones   I

ate washed lettuce from sealed plastic bags
went to parties and rubbed fingers
with strangers

and yet   that wasn't the problem
or it was
only the tiniest part—

you are looking   for the ones behind this, the flaws
in this future; they're here but they won't save you

          pay attention to warm
water slapping your ankles, *who's going*

to tell this story, we say, because we think
the story's ongoing, this is simply an episode, we think
the fires will stop and we'll live

on warm hills made from molten glaciers
and begin again   (and again, again)

The Man

It was grand to borrow the man's
skin, to slide inside his outsides, to finger
his figure open, touch
his eyes. I tried to make his self mine.

The man's hair is a dead animal's,
cold, seeming fake. I try to breathe
into it, but already
it is late autumn: yellow trees,
crows, sun-split clouds.

I had been so angry.
So many abandoned breaths.
I wanted to force something.
Instead I took up the man and
let his blood smear my shoulders.
It was said to be better blood than mine.

The man sang out his images
and I looked through his gore.
It bloodied the brown canal,
hand-sized leaves, a bicycle
stolen all but one wheel.
Everything will vanish, the man said,
this you already know.

But I have not yet felt it. I wait
with the man locked over my shoulders
and I want the dawn
to come faster, surer, and
I want more than this light.

The Fjord in Winter

Getting lost's the best thing I've done, stranded
waist-deep in a fjord at the top of the world,
where rain's pinpricks and scraping gales
meet a gull swooping past a judder of bulldozers
because one day they'll have a sewer here,
and now I see one way's no worse than another.
How we used to think we'd track time with a rope
tie a knot to plot each minute, and never, ever fray.

Let's stop here where the rain cuts
holes through the fjord's face, the light's blunt,
the undercurrent's open to song, slung deep,
as the gull gasps at minuscule crumbs flung out
on flat water. Why not let that gull write our new religion?
We can spend our mornings swooping, cackling,
and then feather our brains out of thought.

The Miracle

What you saw in the sky seemed a sign
that we'd right what had fallen,
that the gleam in the eye of the rat
was not for us, nor the trash that we'd found
in the courtyard built of filth.

We're a lot of us here in the grime.
I thought I'd mended the miracle, darned
it with fingers and thread
while the rat how it watched from its throne
on the heap of empty envelopes, of used hair-dye and the smell
of the blood from the past we had tried to keep back
but the rat knew, and watched,

how its eye knew more than the library
and the letterbox
and the bells of the church spilled through
and were only a rhythm

and still we believed it'd come—
any moment now, the miracle—I hear
it crumbling towards us—
exactly what we deserve.

Exit

Do we begin in death? What kind of building
is a womb, to live inside,
breach the only way through?
The way we watch our mothers later,
unable to keep in our head the thought
of a body fit inside that tiny room.
Is it death in there? Hers
and ours? In the eighteenth century most
died in childbirth so all our luck to wake
in white-panelled hospitals. Last week a friend gave
birth in a room with vast windows
over a small city she adopted. She knew
to ask for the room. I now rent a flat too
large, in the biggest city I've ever lived. Construction
rattles my walls and windows every day. It's a way
of disrupting life's cycles, a way of refusing
nature. I've always wished for a rupture,
to have no final departure,
but these fool verses are still
the only rooms I build.

What's Built Right

You know by the stones. It does. I drank wine till I forgot
each name. I drank wine till I loved. I left you till
you returned. I hated. Hopped from rock to rock and
fell-down-crack. We. Remember, we?
Live on this mangy earthplace. Cracked ourselves open
and loathed. Our loathing, selved. Our selvings, seeped.
I am unloveable; love me. A chirplet, birding.
A baby leaks. We hold our hands too tightly.
As if it could help—it does.

Now, Never

Weak light fjordside, last stop December.

Got a cloud in my chest, and can't
cough it out. Can't unhallow old hollows.

Wind up here turns twigs nodding.
Turns leaves, heads. Why not delay time

to save it for when we're worthy of it,
when we really know how?

Cloud shuffles past its sawdust series.
I wait for you to get here.
Cleaned future. Loosed vowels. Mirror birds

slanting their wings over water. I guess it's now
and never that the fog's bell clangs, the final
bird's wing twists, this jostled

fjord shushes
and our cracked machine
clicks on.

Sunday

Today, around 2am after hearing my friend
vomit in the bathroom after I gave her dinner
she didn't want
following her chemo session, I lie on her sofa bed

trying to pinpoint the centre
of grief or shame or whatever this is

so I can pull out some porcelain plug in my brain
and let each helpless thought drain out.
Come with me back to the door

to listen to her breathing, try to pick up a book,
come back here to this sofa bed—not a shock that tonight
I'm irritated by a British poet's rigid forms
or an American's easeful

abandon. Don't you also wonder
if it's the "I" that makes it so uneasy?
As in, it's my friend who's sick, but how to rip out
my feeling that knows I am not her

but also wants to be her—to take some of *this*
from her and carry it all the way to the coast
and throw it in the bloody sea

—*there's nothing of use to give her*—
anytime we use that clean "I"
let it shine forward so boldly, wearing its
fourteen iambic lines, or its unplanned stanzas

—what does it mean—is it a defence? Is it a
song to stop us remembering
we're all hurtling towards life's last minute?
Grief's all alone—

but also overlapping. When will we know
that the poem can't save us,
or when will we wake up and see how it can?

Mutter

Meaning *mother*, trapped under.
Women, untrap your mother. Let her go after.
Don't wait till she is dead. Hug your mother, hold her.
She is flawed like you,
          and floored by you. She also likes the water,
tucks her hair behind ears
that don't hear like yours but remember
          how you muttered *mama*
those nights she came to you
nights she taught you eight
          o'clock and marbles
and chlorofluorocarbons
while she still had authority
          over your body, and well,
now look at it,
how your skin rumples
blooms and crumples and yes,
how it becomes her.

Held Under

When I got off the plane and got off the phone
and got rid of you, after months of being trapped in
a summer country I couldn't belong in,

how relieved was I to be on my own?

I moved to Berlin, borrowed a life,
a bed, a bike that a friend said
was made for a child. I biked at night

in Neukölln past a long cemetery
and heard women call out
from beyond the stones, and I worried

for each woman anywhere trapped
by a man who wouldn't let her on the
plane, on the phone,

for each woman as if in the wreckage
of an aeroplane, held under scrap metal
by a man who says it'd be cruel

to try to leave. I worry for the women
who're trapped
and I want them to

make their way out, desperately.
Out here is the moon. The roads,
scrawled pages, when you don't have a plan to get home

or you get off at the wrong stop on the subway
and pass under scaffolding to find the pattern
of rain on the bridge is unreadable

to the jagged rhythm of a thousand people's
steps across a city no one's a citizen of

where the collision of unknown languages

is not a list of trappings,
but a series of sturdy escapes.

Apocalypse Next

What country, friends, is this?
It is a changing one, lady,

it will not be the same
next time you step

so do not stop stepping,
never stop lowering

your foot onto the soil, please,
tread sharp through our dreams and out

into this unfathomable wilderness.

What We Find

On our way out here I saw turbines
in the ocean
turning, giant
white crosses among blue

and I do not wish them to be a metaphor for anything.

A man is walking up in a blue t-shirt
ridden up and red shorts
and he believes he is worth listening to.
As I do, clearly, bothering to type.
The water does not believe it is worth listening to.
Can't die or listen.
It continues. We remembered how to sing out here.

A new friend says should I stay in my marriage and I do not
know her well enough to tell her anything except
if you're asking it's not going to be good either way
for a bit. But after a bit there will be the ocean.

Again, the ocean, what's missed here. What gaps
between what we need and what we find.

Resurrection

River's rhythm's ever breaking
(and the notes of our blood
are a call for a song we have heard since

the first stream). A trickle's a kind of terror
halfway between sound and silence; I was up
all night feeling that hum rub inside me,

potential for utter extinction. Longed for
a downpour. All I know is the river's
unworried, unbreathing, and

either one must have been cold a long time
(so the words of a man who has been
long cold might save us)

or else to drown is to turn
the underwater breathable, to face down
into clean cold, inside the finally broken surface.

~

After the Internet

Under this closed shop's awning, freezing,
you dream of it again;
that assemblage of pop stars and lock

smiths, forecasts and breaking
news, Moroccan tiles, flooded supermarkets,
limitless glowing maps.

Now it's gone it's strange to see
how much we held it
close, how we claimed it was our ruin

out of love and need. Taught ourselves how
to never live without it. The big picture's not
been our strong point, your neighbour says, now

all the daily news you have. The newspapers
haven't resumed yet. Your neighbour says
everyone is gathering at the stadium

where it's rumoured the philosophers
will bring us some answers
but when you arrive alone in the city

you've forgotten how the streets clamp together
and as you take too many
wrong turns a storm

blows up fast with those new blue clouds
that pour hail so hard it breaks skin.
Here, stop under this closed shop's awning

and wait for someone to pass
and bring you the words of the philosophers
or at least some clean water and bread.

New Calendar

Which part breaks next? Which town to fall
leaf by leaf, tree by tree, in this crumbling
world? Which thought did you cling to as the guiding
one, the one that would keep the house upright?

Nothing will keep her upright. The weather's
on its way, and her walls rumple like sails.
He laughs, says, whether you weather
the weather has nothing to do with your words.

Wasn't she always doomed?
Is the only way to rewind the catastrophe,
to prevent her from sinking?
Could it be up to you?

Interruption

Let's say you're allowed to live in another era.
Bells, announcing plague.
White church across the way again.
Only at night, footsteps.
Grant me an audience with lace.
Rats, see and know.
Bells sing anew, not now, not now.

Mary Shelley

Gives birth
to a man who gives birth
to a monster, it is morning

on the lake, the poet not yet drowned
when Mary starts the work
of great undrowning

which is to take her life—
still, do not pity her that.
Something always takes your life,

if it's books you're lucky, especially
books on the shore of an impartial lake.
No, the awful part is the loss of the children,

three, unfathomably,
as well as a mother, a husband. Some wonder
she gives birth

to a man who gives birth
to a monster, when it's morning
on the lake, the poet not yet drowned,

the water slick, the book
a glimmer, a stammer,
that glacier unmelted in her gaze.

Twin Peaks

Under the waterfall,
that red room blooms, backwards voices
squeeze through speakers, the TV drips
scenes like blood—ceaselessly,

then stop. For some
years I dated a director
but got tired of being a show.
Got stuck in the nineties, plastic-wrapped

girls, black lodge drapes, they told me
the old bad news when I was taking a splinter
out of my foot, prodding my pink raw
flesh with a needle—wait,

my mother said, wait till she gets it out
(unspoken creature lurking beneath skin)—
but now I remember, they didn't wait,
they went ahead and told me anyway.

I guess I never got it out.

That needle's still in my hand.

Volumnia

We had no use for history but Volumnia's.
That woman against fire.
That mother of a tragic son.
What violence might we unleash through her line?
Oh mother, what have you done?
All the old songs we had nearly forgotten
we now sing in the garden as we wave our torches
and drink to the vastest blazes not lit
to each town not yet in flame.

Cure

I think I'm unstoppable.
Crowds hunt in the streets and still I believe
I won't die, will get through. The panic
in my throat is only of the mild kind, barely more
than a tremor or shudder. I haven't
seen ghosts yet. No woman floating
across buildings, no giant mouth
of a man opening—no, only the fleetingest
glance of shadows, only the irritant
of what's not quite seen.
Will you believe me if I tell you?
I've built a cure for death. I built it
in an attic of a building I don't own.
I wake in the night to dreams of someone
burning down the building. Because although I know
the cure's there, floating
shapeless on that airless top floor
I know I do not own it.
It owns itself. I think myself unstoppable,
but only grow more mortal.
Only the fleetingest glance
of shadows, only the irritant
of what's not quite seen.

After the Catastrophe

I know we're meant to live
in the minute, but what if
that minute snatches us
too sharply, what if we fear
getting caught in it?

I do not like the knife
lying on the carriage floor, waiting.

I do not like how
at each station, new people rise
and say *This is us.*

As if each stop defines them.

Twelve black swans unfurl their wings as a man
waves from a boat called The Gambler.
All strung together by glances.

But what if we made up
that man, those swans,
the boat called The Gambler?
What if we made this entire train,
each fact our eyes quiver past?

After a catastrophe some are
calm the worst is gone.
New people rise
and say *This is us.*

The Lighthouse

Tonight I'm here to tell you that the lighthouse
didn't burn. The gas leaked, glass
broke, walls charred—we woke to an unseen
wound, in this world, this world just as imperfect
as the last. Who listened to the sirens last night
as I ran out from the lighthouse? Who knew
I was too late to stop the gas, too late to put out
the fire that burned down the whole old world?

Still, there's a wonder in reaching this last world,
to stand on the cliff with a blackened lighthouse
still upright and watching the rocks.

Come clamber up here to the last world?
I can offer you water and a concrete slab
to sit on and gaze over these new ruins.
Let's swap stories of the city—
ever-running trains, smiling
public men, millions
of Swedish plywood bookcases—
while we stare out, pour water,
cup our hands, and sip.

Taillight

Windmills stilled in windlessness
no longer creak to shift,
while solar panels still tilt
up to where the sun once blazed.

A short-legged horse appears, lifts her head
to watch you walk by, drops
her head into the long grass.
You should think about eating her, but she was lovely once.
Graffiti reads VORSICHT
on the walls of the empty factory
where every second window's shattered cobwebbed glass.

Wind's stopped, every windmill's stilled

but birds still speak. One taillight ahead on, off; someone else
in this broken place. What you try to do
is make cracked glass into ornament,

turn place to palace. Whether you can see
a path for yourself, on the vehicle with the taillight, across a
railway track; on the short-legged horse, over a river;

whether you see a path through a disused library
or on a boat deck in a city where the pipes still work
and the streets are strangely clean;

whether you see yourself stepping out to stroll
over the surface of the water. Whatever you see, keep
your bones moving, till those windmills creak
and turn.

What Fire

Glimpse to before. Fog rises off the deep fields
like water lifting.
Now the masks appear

as if grown from soil. Found a piece of paper
declaring my grandmother (German,
Jewish) a refugee alien. Who and what is inalienable?

Certainly not a woman. Small autumn trees
crouch under evergreens, is this what you call protection?

*

The fogs are stiff now, touchable. Actual water
forms in our mouth. It isn't
horrifying. We left the city. I never loved it
even when it worked, subways, parties,

celebrities, homeless.
Too much filler, too much matter to reject.
Later we heard fires were moving towards it.

*

The sun burned out is beautiful,
a white circle, you can look right at it, like a round of ash.
Even with the smoke it's clearer out here. I burned
the old things I couldn't look at. People are split:

some say we'll go back almost to before, others say
in no time we'll be suiciding.
They say a man seized control of the city
but what's control of something desperate?

I've never been good at the future. I'll just stay
where I am. It's in the city that the dead are;
here we might never die.
We're learning to catch birds. I caught a cat

and roasted it, after pulling off its skin.

*

It's not, as we say, a world's end, not bang, whimper, not song—
it's just an episode in a series we no longer have writers for.

It's a train ride where the train keeps running
long after it's left the tracks, raging through fields, an angry

steel stallion on fire. It's a story we need in order to live—
or was that in order to die? No matter. You sleep now.

Even fires need to rest.

Earth

When I die I will have learned how not to.
That's what this body's built for, to know
not what it is, to shamble along our stone
floors, sun on back, wondering what to use
this planet for, while it's still

cold enough to walk on. As if it's for us.
As if it always was.
Walk in, walk on, walk through. I swam for all
the generations they gave me. I wrinkled
like a sea-moth. I tried as best I could.
I'm sorry it's not enough.

Das Gift

Hold still. Look down. The camera is remembering
your name; it asks if you will please reveal
your birth. You stare back at your eye: a dried-up
well. Meanwhile, the valleys
see the blossoms' last unfold, watch
the dead blooms fumble on the breeze. One falls
to the gutter by your feet. You lean
to pick its black flesh from the road, listen
for the stirrings of the trees, listen
for the layers of the leaves, aching
for the woods from which they broke. Hold
still. Watch this final season as it turns.

But wait. Look close. The camera has been switched off
at the brain; it's you who's still alive and listening here.
When the curtain fell upon the world, they never taught you
how to save yourself. But here you are without a thing to buy,
and not sure how to build the simplest thing.
You who were estranged from the earth.
Ah well. Walk on!
This story is the best one you've been told, better
than any that they'd sell. Here you are the only one alive!
Once the sewers flooded all the bunkers,
he rich men locked themselves
in frozen tombs. They'd collected all the data that they could
and sold the world back to you at cost.
You bought it, didn't you?
But then they died. Still, if one day, their bodies do defrost,
if they wake and somehow find a way
through all the shit and piss of humankind and into
this future, what will they find?
What will you leave them?

Extinction

Dark already. Too many poems end in fire or light.
If a god were to build
a new world, what would it take from this one?
Is dark needed to recognise light, and if so, what's your

darkness? I choose the winter day in the far far South,
the wind unsurvivable, the ice ready
for its own doom. Too dark to see, no glimpse
of extinction or aurora,
only the wind's hum.

High Water

Just listen, say the dead—listen to what
you call a song but is really a string of
similar notes meant to convey something

beyond a straining for the moon, soil.
Is that a song? say the dead. How do we know
we're alive? The dead tonight

lit up in the water, in the sky, on these streets
lined with birds singing similar strings
of synonymous notes. All so singular, say the dead.

The way you know you're alive, say the
dead, is you waste your time
wondering what makes the living flail.

With the thinness of these islands
in this heat bold as a bell,
how do you live, the dead ask.
By listening to death in the branches.
By hoping the summer will end.

Inland Empire

Weeks after the electricity's out
the sewers stop, and the smell's
putrid paste, rot slop, somehow

death's deletion: as in, it makes an end
seem impossible. Waves turn brown
turn black, and we turn inland

as far as we can from the sea.
Yes, that's why we went, and why
when we got some miles in we sang

with our fingers still over our mouths
sucking in air while keeping most out.
When I say "we" I mean "I."

That's why I live here now and how
the wind sometimes reminds me.
I recall the shame I used to feel—

for not saying the right thing, choosing
the right gift, wearing too little, loving
too much—when the possibilities

for gifts and clothes or
love felt near infinite. How I cried over
what now seems like nothing, and how

now I wish I could do it again, how in the night
I wish for that shame
as if it were a wonder. Now I speak to

the dirt like it's human. And still I don't know
if it's me that's changed, or if it's
only the world.

The River

Each time I try to capture him, I see instead
the ocean I grew up near, or the river we lived by then,
that string of lights I used to count each night
to try to sleep as a child, till my vision slurred
and the string grew to a long, lit line,
his blue eyes sliding on
bootprint-punctured snow, my first time
in Oslo when we hiked
the ski path, as everyone
soared past and we, slow and cobbling
each step, spoke about endings and
philosophers, sky obscenely blue, as we
caught trains, glimpsed mirrors full
of giant buildings being built, improbable
concrete mansions, the river out of sight.

Vanishing Point

Ludicrous to be in love as the world ends,
but that's humans for you, I guess.
The joke's on earth, that we can still
adore while dooming. I wake up
with you and the world seems new.

Incorruptible.
Some people still want to be remembered
forever, even when forever's
never here, or even if it's only
for those last few seconds earth exists, they want
to be left on someone's lips.

It makes no sense to me.
I don't want to vanish
but if we must, I plan to merge myself with you
so that we are two waters swimming amongst
the other, waves forming and fading,
minds gone but water interchangeable,
impossible to evaporate.

What Water Knows

Perhaps what's most surprising is
what won't change, a stubborn straining
in the wave's brain for the sense
that when the last light falls

it will have at last been seen, recognised, gained
access to a castle
of trees that shed
leaves all shades of gold

when the shimmer catches but's
never caught, last light stretched
to rumple the water—
this lake-butter, this bright stutter,
this marriage of light, time, violence—
because all feeds on finitude,
and you will not be sated

as you try to touch what water knows
change and calm, change and calm.

Acknowledgments

Thank you to the editors of the following publications for including poems from this book: *Ambit Magazine, Landfall, The New Republic, Poetry Magazine, Poetry New Zealand, The Poetry Review, Poetry Wales,* and *The Times Literary Supplement.*

Many thanks to everyone who supported this book along the way, including my wonderful editor Deryn Rees-Jones; Alison Welsby and the team at Liverpool University Press; the excellent Mark Leidner, Emily Hasler, Chelsea Wald, and Jeff Doty; and my lovely friends and family. This book is dedicated to Fotini, she of the bike that was made for a child, who has been such an intelligent and crucial friend since our time at the Akademie Schloss Solitude back in 2016. Last and never least, my thanks and love to Eirik Høyer Leivestad, who I'm grateful for every day.